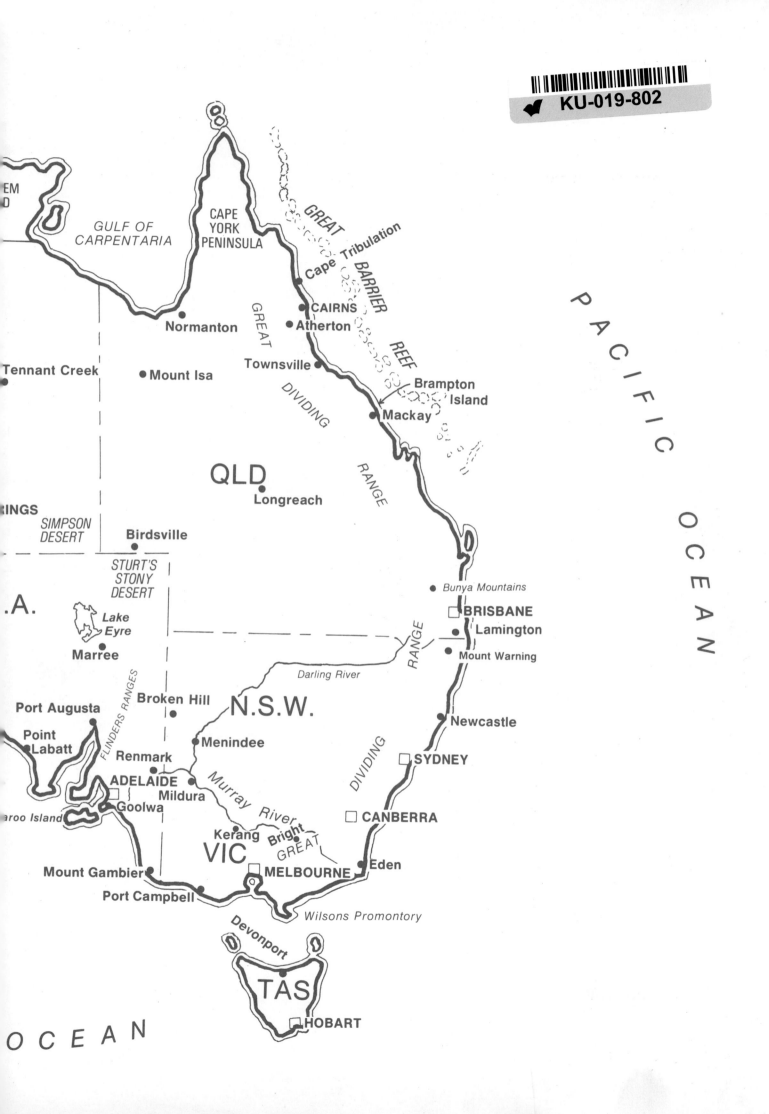

PACIFIC OCEAN

GULF OF CARPENTARIA

CAPE YORK PENINSULA

GREAT BARRIER REEF

Cape Tribulation

CAIRNS
Atherton

Normanton

Townsville

Brampton Island

Mackay

Tennant Creek

Mount Isa

GREAT DIVIDING RANGE

QLD

Longreach

RINGS

SIMPSON DESERT

Birdsville

STURT'S STONY DESERT

.A.

Lake Eyre

Marree

Bunya Mountains

BRISBANE
Lamington

RANGE

Mount Warning

Darling River

FLINDERS RANGES

Broken Hill

N.S.W.

Port Augusta

Point Labatt

Menindee

Newcastle

Renmark

SYDNEY

ADELAIDE
Mildura

Murray River

DIVIDING

CANBERRA

aroo Island

Goolwa

Kerang   Bright

GREAT

Eden

VIC

Mount Gambier

MELBOURNE

Port Campbell

Wilsons Promontory

Devonport

TAS

HOBART

OCEAN

AUSTRALIA
A Special Place

Manning Gorge, the Kimberleys, Western Australia

AUSTRALIA
A Special Place

JOCELYN BURT

RIGBY

ACKNOWLEDGMENTS

I am indebted to many people for their help and assistance in the preparation of this book. In particular I would like to thank Fitz McLean of the Brampton Island Resort; Dick Lang of Desert-Trek Australia, Adelaide; and the National Parks and Wildlife Service of New South Wales.

National Library of Australia
Cataloguing-in-Publication entry

Burt, Jocelyn.
   Australia, a special place.
   ISBN 0 7270 1818 3.
   1. Australia—Description and travel—1976—
   I. Title.

919.4'0463

RIGBY PUBLISHERS • ADELAIDE
SYDNEY • MELBOURNE • BRISBANE • PERTH
NEW YORK • LONDON • AUCKLAND
First published 1983
Copyright © 1983 Jocelyn Burt
All rights reserved
Wholly designed and typeset in Australia
Printed by South China Printing Company, Hong Kong

CONTENTS

Lorne, Victoria

Devil's Marbles, Northern Territory. Situated about 90 kilo-metres south of Tennant Creek, these fascinating rocks lie scattered singly, in groups, and in huge piles over many hectares of land on both sides of the Stuart Highway. They come in all shapes and sizes, all softened or rounded at the edges by erosion

AUSTRALIA: A SPECIAL PLACE

What is it about the world's oldest, flattest, and driest continent that has so much appeal? Largely it is due to the ancient topography, the many unusual animals, birds, and insects, and the abundance of interesting trees and plants. Yet it has something else: a character and atmosphere that is *different*. It is a country full of surprises. At first glance a place may seem to offer little of interest, but when a closer look is taken an infinite diversity is revealed to delight the senses. Those people who know Australia well and return again and again to familiar places are rewarded by an even deeper awareness of its beauty and character.

Much of the topography's character is the result of age. Some land surfaces have been continuously exposed above sea level since the dawn of time—rocks can be seen today that are over 3000 million years old, and unlike other continents, Australia has been relatively free from major earth movements for the last 220 million years. With time well on its side, weathering has had a free hand and has contributed much to the unique and fascinating beauty of this land.

Age and colour are closely linked. Indeed, Australia's natural environment is one of the most colourful on earth. Virtually every colour of the spectrum can be found somewhere in the continent's 4 million square kilometres, ranging from a vivid brilliance to hues so soft and subtle that no artist's paint or photographer's film can do them justice. As it is, people unfamiliar with certain areas often find it hard to believe the colours they *do* see in pictures.

If people are fascinated by Australia's unusual scenery, they are even more intrigued by the wildlife. Although Australians have a great affection for their fauna, many do not realise the extent of the interest among people overseas for our better known animals. Some tourists go mad with excitement at the sight of a kangaroo or Koala in its natural environment. Most species of Australian fauna are unique, with no 'relatives' in other parts of the world. Marsupials gained a stronghold here when they colonised the Australian land mass before it was cut off by the sea from the rest of the ancient continent of Gondwanaland, about 45 million years ago. This allowed them to develop in a region relatively free from predators.

The two most popular marsupials must be the Koala and the kangaroo—the endearing Koala would surely rank with the Chinese panda as the world's most lovable animal. As for kangaroos and their close cousins the wallabies, the sight of a large mob bounding gracefully over the countryside is quite thrilling. Other interesting marsupials include the wombat, numbat, bandicoot, native cat, Tasmanian Devil—a creature related to the native cat, but looking more like a fierce miniature bear—and a variety of possums, kangaroo rats, and mice.

Another popular animal rarely seen except in a few zoos, is the platypus. A monotreme, this semi-aquatic, furry, egg-laying mammal with webbed feet and broad duck-like bill quite baffled a nineteenth-century zoologist, who suggested it was one of the freak objects that wily Chinese taxidermists sold to gullible sailors. Although platypuses are shy creatures, a good place to see them is at dusk in the Broken River at Eungella, near Mackay in Queensland. Sleek, small, and almost mercurial in behaviour, they surface at intervals near the bridge, permitting a frustratingly brief glimpse before disappearing into the water.

One widely appreciated aspect of the Australian bush is that relatively few dangerous creatures live there; consequently it is not necessary to carry a gun. Certainly, some of our snakes are the most poisonous in the world, but people rarely meet these shy reptiles in the wild. There are a couple of species of poisonous spiders, which even the most seasoned bush traveller may never meet—unless he goes looking for them. One of the two species of crocodile in the far north can be extremely dangerous, but usually only when you abuse its territorial rights—by swimming in its waterhole for example.

There are over 700 species of birds of an extraordinary variety, many peculiar to Australia. The assortment of bird calls are as varied as the species, ranging from the musical notes of sheer beauty of the Pied Butcherbird, to the magpies' conversational warble, the raucous screeching of cockatoos and parrots, and the hilarious cackling of the kookaburra. Of all the sounds in the bush, the kookaburra's ringing laugh, so infectiously joyful, is surely the most essentially Australian.

Australia's vegetation is just as interesting as its wildlife. There are many different types of forests which contain magnificent trees, as well as rare plants of great scientific interest. One much-loved tree, the river gum, usually graces paddocks, roadsides, and riverbanks. This wonderful tree is yet another feature that epitomises the character of Australia, and appears in local art more frequently than any other species. The river gum has a potential life-span of 500 years or more, and its often massive, solid trunk is beautifully dressed in mottled bark, supporting strong limbs contoured in every way imaginable—the overall effect being one of distinct grace and individual character.

One of nature's most bountiful gifts to Australia is wildflowers. They often provide a tremendous contrast to their environment— which may be harsh deserts, craggy hillsides, rugged gorges, or evergreen forests and woodlands. Found in a wide range of habitats, most species (approximately 15 000) are indigenous to this country, and new varieties are being discovered each year. Many are unique in form too. Sturt's Desert Pea, with its flower reaching 10 centimetres in length is like a blood-red exclamation mark, and 'Kangaroo Paw' and 'Cat's Paw' really are apt names. The bottlebrushes, fat, candle-like banksias, many kinds of paper daisies, and the intriguing carnivorous plants all provide endless enchantment. There are over 600 species of orchids, many of them exquisitely beautiful. By far the richest wildflower regions lie in the scrubby sand plains of Western Australia, which become wild gardens blazing with colour after rain. Perhaps the most astonishing wildflower settings are the deserts, when a long, dry spell is broken by drenching rains and the barren wastes are carpeted with an incongruous profusion of flowers.

Although much of Australia's beauty is grand and demands admiration, it is also characterised by a stark, almost elusive simplicity. This may appear in the sun setting behind some ancient, rounded boulders in central Australia, or in a sand-dune, rippled by the wind, that rises in pristine splendour from a desert plain, or when a dead tree is silhouetted against a glistening, white salt-pan. A strange, almost weird beauty is evoked when the last rays of light fall on the stony ruins of the abandoned homesteads, pubs, and telegraph stations of the Outback. Silent testimonies to heartbreaking droughts and unfulfilled dreams, these sad ruins are chilling reminders that much of Australia is harsh country, intolerant of the weak.

The dusty Outback ruins are in striking contrast to the towns and villages nestling in the foothills of the green mountains in eastern Australia, where life-giving rains frequently wash roofs and tree-lined streets, and nourish gardens, fields, and streams. Here the beauty is one of refreshing softness. Sometimes in the early mornings on fine days there is even a hint of delightful mystery, when the lazily drifting mists, snowy white in the first sunlight, play hide-and-seek with the mountains surrounding the towns. There are many scenes similar to this one which remind us that Australia possesses much to gladden hearts. A land of extraordinary contrasts and unique character, it is indeed a special place.

River gums, Flinders Ranges, South Australia. These gums line Moralana Creek; the Elder Range can be seen in the distance. A lovely scenic drive of 28 kilometres runs past here, linking the Leigh Creek Road in the west, to the Wilpena–Blinman Road in the east

Pelicans at Lake Curalo, Eden, New South Wales. Always in hope of a feed, these birds will come in close to the water's edge when fishermen are cleaning their catch. Eden lies on the south coast of New South Wales, just over the Victorian border

Kangaroo and joey. There are about fifty species in this family, including wallabies, rat and tree kangaroos. The larger kangaroos have been known to keep pace with a car travelling at 50 kilometres an hour. If they are chased hard enough, the young are tossed from the females' pouches; not in order to save the baby, but rather because the pouch muscles become tired

Ruins of the old telegraph station at Strangways, lying south
of Oodnadatta. Nearby are some small thermal springs, known
as the Strangways Springs; like many in the region, they are
gradually drying out

Bright, Victoria. One of the loveliest small towns in Australia, Bright nestles in the Ovens Valley at the foothills of the Victorian Alps, 300 kilometres north-east of Melbourne. Here the town is partially blanketed in an early morning autumn mist

THE GREAT OUTBACK

Australia's Outback is the vast, arid land that lies well beyond the coastal cities and the green mountain slopes of the east, encompassing more than three-quarters of the continent. This is the region that reflects Dreamtime magic and the genesis of time in its stark and strangely beautiful landscapes. It is an area that captures the imagination and thrills the soul, that irresistibly draws people to experience its uniqueness.

The Outback is a land of plains, deserts, and rugged rocky ranges slashed with marvellous gorges, gaps, and chasms. More often than not its rivers and streams are filled with sand, not water. By contrast, its northernmost regions are part of the tropics. In the Outback's 'Dead Heart' lie the great monoliths of Ayers Rock, the Olgas, and Chambers Pillar. Colour dominates here to a degree seen nowhere else in Australia: no scene is the same in the morning or afternoon, at sunrise or sunset, for the land responds superbly to the capricious changes of directional light.

For some people, the deserts and vast plains are boring, and scream of dullness; others enjoy the refreshing, uncluttered simplicity conducive to freedom and spiritual peace. Many people are fascinated by the amazing diversity of the deserts: vast stretches of scrubby wasteland, or areas patched with blinding white salt-pans and gridded with dunes that march unbroken for hundreds of kilometres. Sands may be any shade between white, yellow, and red. The most forbidding deserts are the stony wastes, seas of gibbers varying in size from tiny pebbles to stones bigger than footballs.

There are six major deserts. Three of them, the Great Sandy, the Gibson, and the Great Victoria converge to form a huge wasteland, covering a good portion of Western Australia and extending into South Australia. South Australia also has Sturt's Stony Desert and much of the Simpson Desert, which runs into Queensland and the Northern Territory. The Territory's other major desert is the Tanami.

The Simpson Desert is the most interesting, and certainly the most challenging for motorists. Covering an area of around 140 000 square kilometres, the colourful red dunes are fixed in longitudinal ridges that rise to heights of up to 45 metres. As the western aspect of each dune is much steeper than the eastern approach, crossings are usually made from west to east. No roads cross the desert, but to the south a network of old and often faint tracks left by geologists remain for experienced Outback travellers to follow if they prefer not to cut their own trails. An H.F. radio and all possible provisions, including water, *must* be carried. In years of good seasonal rains, the Simpson is transformed into a superb natural garden, full of interesting flowering plants. There is plenty of wildlife too, and travellers usually see dingoes, feral camels, and a variety of reptiles and birds. At the western edge, near Dalhousie, the spectacular Purni Bore, with its strange mineral formations and billowing steam, seems more like a New Zealand thermal spring than an Australian waterhole.

The sands of the Simpson gradually give way to the gibbers of Sturt's Stony Desert, which lies chiefly between the Diamantina River and Cooper Creek in north-eastern Australia. The explorer Charles Sturt, who was the first to cross it in 1845, correctly summed up the nature of this desert when he commented, 'A country such as I firmly believe has no parallel on the earth's surface.' Not all of it is stone, for in parts the gibbers give way to areas of spinifex and red sand.

One of the joys of all red sand-dunes in Australia is that at sunrise and sunset they change to hills of blood-red splendour, as the sun balances on the horizon. Other beautiful dunes of a more conventional sandy colour lie in the vicinity of the Birdsville Track, which runs between Birdsville in Queensland and Marree in South Australia. In those rare years when Cooper Creek floods this area, the water carves a passage through the sand, lending the dunes edging the creek an exceptional beauty.

Rising abruptly from the Outback plains in a number of areas are the ranges, often comprising a series of craggy, worn-looking elevations. Only two series have any notable height, and they are

Mount Sonder, Northern Territory. The second highest mountain in the MacDonnell Ranges, it is a prominent landmark in the far western section of the ranges

the Flinders Ranges in South Australia, and the MacDonnell Ranges in central Australia.

The Flinders Ranges rise in gentle hills around Crystal Brook, 200 kilometres north of Adelaide, although many tourists think of them as starting about 110 kilometres north of Pichi Richi Pass, near Quorn. Unlike many of the interesting Outback areas, the Flinders are relatively close to the densely populated south-eastern portion of Australia, and access via good roads is easy. Once there, however, care must be taken on some of the unsealed roads, which become impassable after rain. This area is one of the best-loved in Australia, and most people need little excuse to go there. There is a quality that is essentially Australian, indeed, almost emotive, in the profusion of magnificent river gums that line creeks and roads, and stand proudly against backdrops of softly rounded hills and higher rugged ranges. Beauty is everywhere, and nearly every road and track lying between Wilpena Pound and the Parachilna area could be called a 'scenic route.'

Serpentine Gorge, Northern Territory. Lying 4 kilometres off the Alice Springs–Glen Helen Road, this small but beautiful gorge captures the essential character of the many gorges in the MacDonnell Ranges. Glowing all shades of red and brown, the sheer, craggy walls coolly shelter graceful gums and a pebbly creek.

The MacDonnell Ranges, flanking Alice Springs to the east and west, are sheer exhilaration, and provide many brilliantly coloured scenic treasures. Even if the visitor's time is limited, the western MacDonnells should not be missed—no visit to central Australia is complete without seeing the MacDonnell's Mount Sonder at dawn. The second highest mountain in these ranges, rising to 1346 metres, it is a notable landmark in the country around Glen Helen, 130 kilometres from Alice Springs. It can easily be viewed from the hill near the Glen Helen Chalet. Heralding the sun's re-appearance, while all the surrounding land is still veiled in dark shadows, Mount Sonder becomes a poem of pinks and mauves. But this delectable beauty is brief; as the sun climbs higher in the sky, the colours are chased away by the strengthening light.

Immediately after viewing this spectacle, take a walk to the nearby Glen Helen Gorge. By now the sun will have turned the magnificent walls that rise like great battlements over the Finke River a fiery red. If there is water in the river and no breeze, the

Cooper Creek, near Kopperamanna Crossing at the Birdsville Track. Many lovely sand-dunes line the Cooper between Lake Hope and the old Killalpaninna mission ruins

entire scene will be dramatically reflected. Sometimes the pool blocks the gorge entrance, preventing access to the equally beautiful reflections in the scenic area beyond.

The biggest drawcard in central Australia is Uluru National Park, home of Ayers Rock and the Olgas. These two celebrated landforms rank among the great natural wonders of the world; they are also sacred symbols of the Aboriginal Dreamtime legends. Ayers Rock is the biggest single piece of exposed rock on the earth's surface, with a circumference of 9·5 kilometres and a height of 348 metres rising dramatically above a vast plain. Most people visiting the Rock for the first time are not prepared for its gigantic, awe-inspiring size, and are generally more conscious of its magnitude than anything else. On subsequent visits, without losing this sense of awe, they are more aware of the monolith's superb detail than of its size.

Walking around the base of the Rock is a delight, especially in the Maggie Spring area. The visitor can begin to understand its marvellous character, for this close view shows the incredible indentations and stained fissures, the rock holes, caves, and fallen boulders, the plant and bird life. Climb-

The Finke River, Glen Helen, Northern Territory. Late afternoon, upstream from the chalet and the gorge. Exploration is especially enjoyable when long pools of water, left over from the last flood, mirror the surroundings

ing the Rock has become very 'fashionable', and is a particularly rewarding experience if your are fit; for those who are not, or who, for some unfathomable reason insist on climbing in high-heeled shoes and tight skirts, it must be a nightmare. The record number of climbs made by one person in one day is said to be twenty-seven—although anyone who has climbed Ayers Rock would find this rather hard to believe!

The other main attraction is the sunset, which is commonly viewed from an area known as Sunset Strip, lying well beyond the Rock. However at close range the colours seem richer, and proximity to those magnificent walls as they blaze red as if on fire brings a deeper awareness of their fantastic beauty. Both the Rock and the Olgas undergo wonderful colour changes through reds, browns, and purples during the day, as the direction of light varies. If clouds are present at sunrise or sunset, the colours are more intense. Should the sun come out after rain, the monoliths shine like gun-metal.

Many people say the Olgas are more interesting than Ayers Rock. The two should never be com-

A salt-pan near the Approdinna Attora Knolls, Simpson Desert. Generally the salt covers firm ground and provides a pleasantly smooth surface to drive over—a change from the rough sandy terrain of the desert. However, in wet years the pans can be treacherous, hiding a veritable water table beneath them

pared, because each has its own distinctive beauty and character. Lying 32 kilometres west of Ayers Rock, the Olgas' extraordinary collection of over thirty domes, fashioned by the elements and set in a circle, are geologically distinct from the Rock— though both are sandstone and were formed over 500 million years ago. Each dome is separated by a ravine, which supports a surprising amount of plant

life, sustained by moisture trapped in gullies.

There are many good walks, and to appreciate the Olgas, you need to take several. Walking in ravines such as the Valley of the Winds and Mount Olga Gorge, shows the rough, conglomerate walls that are studded with a million varieties of pebbles; there is a strange sensation when looking up at the tops of the sheer, towering walls, which appear to loom ominously over everything. A walk around the perimeter (for example, the four-wheel-drive track running beyond the Mount Olga Gorge turn-off) provides quite a different perspective of the domes. Best of all, the grand finale is the relatively easy climb to Katatjuta Lookout to see one of

Ayers Rock, Northern Territory. Veiled in late afternoon shadows, this monolith lies in grandeur in the Uluru National Park, 426 kilometres south-west of Alice Springs. For the European Ayers Rock is a unique tourist attraction; for the Aboriginal it is the setting for Dreamtime legends and myths

Australia's great panoramas: a view of all the domes. The best time is at dawn or shortly after, when the domes across the inner valley, partly veiled in shadows, stand out boldly in relief.

Western Australia's two most well-known Outback regions are the Pilbara and the Kimberleys. Both are quite different from the central Australian landscape. The Pilbara's Hamersley Range, a national park lying in rugged ironstone country, is agape with brilliantly coloured gorges that visitors commonly view from above. This can be a terrifying experience for people who don't like heights, for in some places the sheer walls plummet to 150 metres. Splashed with rusts and reds, the vivid chocolate walls of these great chasms strongly accentuate the clean, white trunks of the eucalypts and the domes of yellow spinifex that top the range's plateau. Kinder to the senses are the landscapes around Wittenoom, the small town nestling at the foot of the range. If the seasonal rains have been good, the wildflowers splash even more colour around, and sometimes great candelabras of mulla-mullas carpet the plains right up to the folds of the range.

Ayers Rock at sunset. Although the most popular area for viewing a sunset lies well beyond the Rock, it is far more rewarding to stand near the walls when they are fired red by the setting sun. This is near the climbing area

In the far north-west of Western Australia lie the Kimberleys, comprising a series of worn ranges and an ancient, dissected plateau that was once a coral reef under an ancient sea. Drenched by tropical rains for four months of the year, and baked mercilessly by an unbearably hot sun for the other eight, this inhospitable yet wildly beautiful corner of the continent is still very much 'last frontier country.' Much of it is inaccessible to vehicular and foot traffic, despite the impact of recent mining activities and the upgrading of beef roads. Even in the dry winter months it presents a challenge for travellers, both physically and mentally, but the experience is rewarding, for this is one place in Australia which still has many secrets to reveal. To fully understand this region, one should experience a wet season, when the land pulsates with new life and freshness. During the 'dry' the scenery is passive, as if its character lies dormant, waiting for the violent storms and heavy rains to roll in and awaken it.

If travellers find the colours of the Centre and the Pilbara exciting, they will be overwhelmed by the Kimberleys. It is like stepping into a vivid oil

The Olgas from Katatjuta Lookout, Northern Territory. The highest dome is Mount Olga, rising to 546 metres. The easiest to climb is Katatjuta Lookout; other summits are accessible but difficult to climb—especially Mount Olga

painting. With its thrilling, often dramatic scenery, this area is guaranteed to send photographers and artists wild with joy. Places like Windjana and Geikie gorges near Fitzroy Crossing are steeped in beauty and atmosphere. Manning and Barnett river gorges, lying off the Gibb River beef road, shelter lush tropical vegetation and crystal clear water-holes. In low light these gorges truly come into the fullness of their beauty, when their chunky walls turn a vibrant orange and are reflected deeply in the water.

Without doubt, the finest sunsets in the Outback are seen around the lagoons and billabongs in the Top End of the Northern Territory—especially those in the Kakadu National Park, lying immediately west of Arnhem Land. As monsoon clouds build up towards the end of the dry season, the sunsets are likely to be highly dramatic. This, together with the palls of smoke that hang in the air after the excessive burning-off undertaken during the 'dry', make the sight of the sun, an immense, glowing orb floating on the horizon in a film of haze, truly wonderful.

The Outback's beauty does not end at sunset. No matter where you are—in the deserts, on the plains, near a range, or in a gorge—the nights are very special. Awestruck, one watches the huge, diamond-studded sky displaying clouds of stars seldom seen in the cities—stars that seem to press in close, yet at the same time give a tremendous sense of space. Above all, one is aware of the silence, a profound, cathedral-like peace.

Hamersley Range, near Wittenoom, Western Australia. Lying 1450 kilometres north of Perth, this ironstone range is renowned for its chocolate-coloured gorges and harshly beautiful terrain. The wildflowers in the foreground are Mulla-Mullas—sometimes known as Pussytails (*Ptilotus* sp.)

Windjana Gorge, Western Australia, at dawn. Situated near Fitzroy Crossing in the Kimberleys, Windjana's massive limestone walls tower over the long pools left after the last annual flooding of the Lennard River. In the dry season these pools will disappear. This permanent waterhole is home for a number of harmless Johnstone River Crocodiles which can often be seen floating on the surface like a collection of knobbly sticks

Chichester Range, Western Australia. This national park lies between Wittenoom and Roebourne, in the Pilbara. The Roebourne Road runs through the park for many kilometres, passing high over the colourful ridgetops, in places so littered with stones that it seems a giant tiptruck has been at work

Kakadu National Park, Northern Territory. One of the best places at the top of the Territory to see a sunset is at Yellow Water Lagoon, a backwater of the Jim Jim Creek. These waters are excellent for fishing, particularly just before and after the wet season, at around sunrise and sunset. Kakadu is now one of Australia's major national parks, covering an area of 6000 square kilometres immediately west of Arnhem Land

HIGH COUNTRY

In a country where the average elevation is about 300 metres, it is only natural that many of Australia's ranges and higher peaks are classed as mountains when, strictly speaking, they are really no more than hills compared to the great mountains of the world. As the Australian land mass was formed so early in the geological history of the world, the elements have had ample time to erode the results of the last of the great mountain upheavals without further interruption. Seen from the air, most of the ranges are either worn stumps, or a series of gentle folds, rather crumpled and creased.

Their great age is to our advantage. Many of our mountains' peaks and slopes are much more accessible than those of their mighty overseas counterparts. Not that Australia's mountain ranges should be taken lightly by anyone; there are many steep escarpments, wild, rugged gorges, and bold, jagged cliffs to challenge the most experienced mountaineer. Slopes are often covered in forests where it is easy to become lost, and the weather on our mountains can be unpredictable. However, many Australians find it enormously satisfying to be able to walk instead of climb with ropes and grappling irons to the summit of Mount Kosciusko, the country's highest mountain, and to calmly explore the lovely trails leading to Mount Bogong and Mount Feathertop, Victoria's highest peaks.

The backbone of Australia is the forest-clad Great Dividing Range. The only continental mountain chain in the country, the Great Divide as it is generally called, lies in the east and consists of a series of ranges, plateaux, and spurs that stretch for over 4000 kilometres from Cape York in the far north, to Victoria and Tasmania in the south. Separating the fertile coastlands from the vast Outback, it is a vital watershed for nearly half the continent. The Great Divide is remarkable for its greatly varied climate and landscape. The traveller can follow the range from the balmy atmosphere of a lush tropical rainforest in northern Australia, where the air is warm and enervating and sunlight filters softly through shady canopies of green leaves,

through to the dazzling white world of the southern snow fields. Here cold winds stir the gums burdened with snow, and alpine lakes and tarns lie covered with ice.

Many people overseas are surprised to learn that Australia has snow in winter, which for a few brief months covers an area larger than Switzerland. The highest land mass found in this region is the Snowy Mountains, rising in wild splendour in south-eastern New South Wales. Here peaks reach heights of over 2000 metres, the highest being Mount Kosciusko at 2228 metres. Known collectively as the Australian Alps, they extend into the north-eastern corner of Victoria, where the highest peak, at 1983 metres, is Mount Bogong.

Where there is snow, there are skiers, and increasing numbers of people are discovering the joy of jetting down a white slope to the sound of swishing skis. Australia was one of the first countries to make it a sport, when it was introduced by some Scandinavian miners in the 1860s to help pass away the time in the snowbound gold town of Kiandra, in the Snowy Mountains. Since then a number of ski resorts both in New South Wales and Victoria have been developed to international standards, despite the fact their runs are generally shorter in length than those in Europe and America.

Although the ski runs are shorter, the opportunities for cross-country skiing are almost limitless. As popular as downhill skiing is in this country, it is expensive, and both crowded slopes and long queues at the tows are resulting in more people turning to ski touring. The high plains around Victoria's Mount Feathertop and Mount Hotham, as well as the Bogong High Plains at Falls Creek, are ideal for this, and offer some of the finest winter alpine scenery in the country. The distant views of snow-capped mountains and ridges are breathtaking, but even more captivating is the beauty enjoyed at close range by the skier. On some days it is like passing through a fantasy wonderland. After a blizzard the windward side of every protruding branch and twig is laden with wind-driven ice, or glassy mounds are briefly

Falls Creek, Victoria. Situated 378 kilometres from Melbourne and only three-quarters of an hour's drive from the alpine town of Mount Beauty in the Kiewa Valley, this resort offers some of the best skiing in Australia. The slopes rise as high as 1800 metres, and are dotted with many ski tows

Bogong High Plains, Victoria. Each blizzard leaves its icy signature on the windward side of branches and sticks on the alpine high plains and mountain tops

sculpted into fantastic shapes. After a fresh fall of snow the gums are powdered white, and when the branches become too heavily laden, waterfalls of snow tumble to the ground. On days when the wind moves through the trees, the silence of the plain is broken by the sound of frozen gum leaves tinkling like charms on a bracelet.

In summer the alps invite exploration. It is the time for wildflowers, and the cool sunny days are ideal for walking. The Kosciusko National Park has many good walks, and one of the best leads to the summit of Mount Kosciusko. Now that the last 8 kilometres of the summit road have been closed,

the easiest way to the top is via the Thredbo chair-lift, which links up with the walking track to the summit road, making it a round trip of about 10 kilometres. With its boulder-strewn slopes that give way to stark, bare ranges, the Mount Kosciusko area has a much deeper atmosphere of wilderness than the soft beauty of the Victorian Alps. Nonetheless, it is exhilarating to stand on Kosciusko's summit, the roof of Australia, even when threatening clouds pour in from the south at unbelievably fast speeds, and the wind blows so fiercely it makes photography almost impossible.

Still wilder alpine country lies in south-west Tasmania, the island State off the coast of Victoria. Of all Australia's mountains, those in Tasmania most closely resemble classic alpine scenery. With serrated ridges and jagged peaks rearing above

Hotham Heights, Victoria. Near the Mount Loch car park a meadow of daisies stretches towards the Razorback Ridge, with Mount Buffalo in the far distance. In summer the high plains and mountain tops support a surprisingly rich variety of flora; many species are not found elsewhere in the State. Hotham Heights, an hour's drive from Bright, is a good place to be on a hot, sunny day, because the temperature is 10 degrees cooler than in the valley below

glacial lakes and rugged plateaux, this area forms part of an extensive and wildly beautiful wilderness. One of the most exciting places for bush walkers is Cradle Mountain, part of a national park in the Central Highlands, extending to Lake St Clair in the south. The two places are linked by an 80-kilometre walking track, which is Australia's answer to the famous Milford Track in New Zealand. There is also a network of well-marked trails meandering around Cradle Mountain and through the lovely beech forests. Rising in grandeur over Dove Lake and a number of smaller neighbouring tarns, the distinctive silhouette of Cradle Mountain dominates most of the walking paths, giving the area an awesome atmosphere. Once you start exploring Cradle Mountain it is very hard to stop. The weather is often downright inclement, but this only adds to the beauty and atmosphere. The character of the scenery is changing constantly: one minute swirling clouds drape the peaks in greyness, the next they lift to reveal the dramatic contours of the mountain.

From the slopes of Mount Kosciusko, New South Wales. Only a few hour's drive from Canberra, it is Australia's highest mountain, rising to 2228 metres. There is some excellent walking around these slopes in the summer months

Whenever the sun comes out from behind heavy clouds, the moist vegetation sparkles brilliantly; but intermittently grey curtains of rain will sweep over the land. A photographer may wait a week or so for a clear day; when it finally arrives, the sun may only shine for a few hours. The weather rather than the terrain is the greatest hazard for hikers — even in summer, snow and severe storms can suddenly move in. It is essential for all walkers to register their routes with the rangers.

Both in Tasmania and mainland Australia the mountain roads are constantly being improved, and it is now possible to view good scenery from the car — though of course motorists miss so much by *not* walking. One of the grandest vistas in the Great Dividing Range is easily accessible by car: the Three Sisters in the Blue Mountains at Katoomba, west of Sydney. Rising over 450 metres above forested slopes, these towers of weathered sandstone are a marvellous sight at sunset, when they turn a rich gold. The Blue Mountains were named for the striking hue they take when viewed from a distance.

North of the Blue Mountains there are a number of interesting high areas. The Barrington–Gloucester

Stirling Range, Western Australia. Rising abruptly over the sand plains in the south-west of the State, here one of the peaks of the Stirling Range is wrapped in cloud at sunset. This range, situated about 90 kilometres north of Albany, is a national park famed for its spring wildflowers. The highest peak, Bluff Knoll, rising to 1109 metres, is sometimes capped with snow in winter

Tops region, a plateau forming a south-eastern spur of the Great Divide, lies about 54 kilometres from Tamworth. Here rapids and waterfalls drop dramatically into deep gorges, and forests shelter many species of trees, including the Antarctic Beech. Dominating the Tweed Valley in the far north-eastern corner of New South Wales is the distinctive peak of Mount Warning, an ancient volcanic plug dominating the rainforested slopes of the mountain below. The walk to the top of the plug is a good one, and from the summit's miniature plateau—measuring all of thirty-five footsteps across—one can discover incredible views at all points of the compass.

In Queensland, south-west of Brisbane and the Gold Coast lie the McPherson Ranges. The roads winding up to some of the plateaux are narrow and very steep, but well worth the drive. Near Springbrook are the Purling Brook falls, which drop 107 metres over the sheer escarpment. A lovely 4-kilometre walking path winds down to the bottom of the falls, then passes under the great curtain of water itself, and up the other side. Walking under the falls is safe if there is no wind to blow the water back on the rock face. When this happens, the tumbling water hits the path and anyone unfortunate enough to be on it. Generally the wind comes in bursts, and it is possible to race across in a lull, only getting slightly damp in the mist.

The most well-known plateau in this area is Lamington, topping a spur of the McPherson Ranges. Lying on the Queensland–New South Wales border, this national park is bound by spectacular escarpments rising to 900 metres and more, and contains a wealth of beauty in its rainforests, peaks, bluffs, gorges, and high mountain streams that give way to over 500 waterfalls. From the edge of the plateau there are superb aerial-like vistas over the Great Dividing Range. On a clear day, from the

eastern rim, it is possible to see the rollers of the Pacific Ocean, with the high-rise buildings of the Gold Coast standing like tiny matchsticks against the blue sea. It is hardly surprising that this entire border region is known as the 'Scenic Rim'.

Queensland's highest mountain is the rainforested Mount Bartle Frere, rising to 1612 metres, with Bellenden Ker not far behind at 1593 metres. Both these mountains preside over the Atherton Tableland, a large plateau of the Great Dividing Range, covering a wide area from the Palmer River on Cape York Peninsula to the headwaters of the Burdekin River beyond Ingham. The granite peaks of these two mountains are very rugged, and rainforest grows only in the spots sheltered by rocks. All other vegetation is stunted due to the strong, pruning winds. At this high, tropical altitude, where the summits of the mountains are frequently shrouded in mist and rain, a number of rare plant species, including Australia's only native rhododendron find a perfect environment.

Cradle Mountain, Tasmania. The mountain lies at the end of Dove Lake, which was gouged by glacial action millions of years ago. Part of a large national park situated in the central Tasmanian highlands, Cradle Mountain is 80 kilometres from Devonport

An old snow gum, Dargo High Plains, Victoria. These trees grow in woodlands and thickets in the alpine country of New South Wales, Victoria, and Tasmania between 1370 and 1676 metres above sea-level. In the summer months cattle are brought up to the Dargo High Plains to graze on the lush grass among the snow gums

The Three Sisters, Katoomba, New South Wales. This is one of the most popular vistas in the Great Dividing Range, and the best time to see it is at sunset, when the sandstone flares a deep gold. Katoomba lies in the part of the Great Divide known as the Blue Mountains. This area presented a formidable barrier for western expansion in the early days—it was twenty-five years before the first settlers were able to find a way over them

IN THE FORESTS

Nowhere can one find such refreshing beauty as in the cool, quiet, and verdant forests. Majestic trunks stand like great gothic pillars, their leaves, twigs, and branches forming a million mosaic patterns against the sky. Forests are the cathedrals of nature —centuries old and deserving much respect.

It is impossible to gauge the beauty and interest of forests from the outside—when they are seen from a distance they appear monotonously the same. Walking among the trees, you discover just the opposite. Often the trees' quiet appearance hides an enormous amount of activity, for a host of living creatures reside there.

Australia possesses many diverse rainforests including sclerophyll forests and woodlands. Many of them are unique. They are among our most valuable natural assets, yet they are probably the most abused: either by foresters, foolish governments, and land developers, or by vandals and firebugs. Just as alarming is the widespread loss of trees through the depredations of leaf-eating beetles and the disease 'dieback'—caused by the introduced Cinnamon Fungus. Even before the arrival of the Europeans, there was very little forested land in relation to the size of the continent. When the first settlers arrived, forest covered only 15 per cent of the country; today it covers only 5 per cent, a figure which continues to shrink. In the early years there was virtually no protection, and large tracts of trees were cleared indiscriminately for agriculture and the timber industry; 200 years later many people wonder if the situation is much improved.

Of all the forests, the rainforest in north-eastern Australia is the most threatened. The tragedy is that once destroyed, this type of forest can never grow to be the same again, because it takes millions of years for its unique ecosystem to develop. There are various types of rainforest in Australia: monsoonal, tropical to sub-tropical, and temperate. The monsoonal types are confined to the northern

Purling Brook Falls, Queensland. These falls are part of the Gwongorella National Park

areas of Cape York Peninsula, and their very remoteness affords some degree of protection. The tropical and sub-tropical varieties stretch from the lower portion of Cape York Peninsula to northern New South Wales. Pockets of temperate rainforest are found from New South Wales through Victoria to Tasmania.

Some of the national parks on the Atherton Tableland behind Cairns have become prime tourist attractions because of the rainforests they protect. Well-made paths meander through tropical vegetation, where orchids hide shyly in trees and behind rocks, and colourful fungi add gaiety to the lush greenness of the scene; mosses and lichens festoon trunks and branches, vines twist, coil, and grip anything in their reach, and fountains of ferns spill over boulders, other plants, and near the walking tracks. Although Strangler Fig Trees are a common sight in most rainforests, the 'Curtain Fig Tree' lying in a pocket of rainforest near Yungaburra is spectacular. The Strangler Fig starts life as a tiny seed dropped in the fork of a tree by birds. The seed then sends down aerial roots that grow in lattice fashion around the host's trunk, often causing it to die of strangulation. But if the host is a leaning tree—like the one at Yungaburra—the fig's aerial roots are deprived of a stronghold and will grow into a dense curtain instead.

There are many other intriguing features unique to rainforests. A few trees bear flowers and fruit which sprout directly from the trunk and main branches, a phenomenon known as cauliflory: good examples of this can be seen in the Crater National Park, and beside the Daintree River at the punt crossing. Another fascinating sight is the buttresses, the strange, fin-like panels of wood growing out from the tree's base, which are believed to be part of the root system. Buttresses are not confined to particular types of trees; certain species in all major tree families have them. Many grow to a metre or more in height, like those found on trees at Mount Warning in northern New South Wales; occasionally they grow to mammoth proportions—there is one in Iron Range, south of Cape York, where the panels

Above:
Mountain Ash forest (*Eucalyptus regnans*), Victoria. The Maroondah Highway between Healesville and Marysville runs through some lovely Mountain Ash forest, which also shelters many tree ferns. The trees here are very young—this section of forest was replanted after savage bushfires swept through in 1939

Left:
Sub-tropical rainforest, Mount Warning, New South Wales. Once a tree falls in the rainforest, the process of decomposition quickly sets in. Through the action of fungi, insects, and hordes of bacteria, this log will gradually become the humus which feeds other plants. A well-graded track zig-zags through this forest up to Mount Warning's summit, which offers a wonderful panoramic view of the north-eastern corner of New South Wales

Fan Palms, north Queensland. This unusually large grove of Fan Palms lies deep in a tropical rainforest near Cape Tribulation, north of Cairns. Their true beauty is seen on looking up to the forest's canopy, when the sunlight filtering through the leaves accentuates their intricate patterns

are at least 6 metres high, giving the tree the appearance of a rocket resting on its launching pad.

The methuselahs of the rainforests are the Antarctic Beeches. These increasingly rare relics of an Ice Age first appeared 50 million years ago, and are now found only in a few pockets at high altitudes of the Great Dividing Range between the McPherson Ranges and the Barrington–Gloucester Tops region. The best place to see them is in the Lamington National Park, along the beautiful border track near O'Reilly's. Here they dominate the forest with their gnarled trunks and limbs thickly draped in green moss. They are the finest stands in Australia, and forestry experts believe them to be around 3000 years old.

Another species of beech, Myrtle Beech, is the most common tree in Tasmania's cool temperate rainforests. These forests are exquisitely beautiful, reminiscent of scenes from old European fairy tales, such as *Hansel and Gretel*. Sheltering under a lacy canopy of tiny myrtle leaves, the beech forest is a damp world where moss and lichen cover twisted

Here colourful fungi grows on a rotting log, adding brightness to the gloomy light of a rainforest's floor in Queensland

roots and old logs, and hang from twigs and branches like Christmas decorations. In places these forests grow right down to the coast, but much of this terrain is inaccessible. In the Cradle Mountain–Lake St Clair National Park many walking tracks cut through these forests. For people not keen on long walks, the Cradle Mountain's Waldheim Chalet car park is situated only a few metres from a beech forest.

The eucalypts—known as gum trees—are the most prevalent trees in Australian forests, and large tracts of them cover the mountains and ranges; indeed, eucalypts more than any other tree make a scene uniquely Australian. One of the delights of these forests is the mixture of strong scents released from the eucalypt oils, flowers, and grasses, accentuated by the heat of a summer's day; at night the aromas take on a special freshness. In spring, one of the most powerful and sweet-smelling scents comes from the flowering acacias—the wattles. With brilliant yellow blooms dripping from them like golden rain, the wattles herald the new season. Another interesting feature of the eucalypt forests is the variety of tree-bark. It can be smooth or rough, mottled, or simply a uniform white, salmon pink, brown, or grey. Sometimes great ribbons of

Above:
Antarctic Beech trees (*Nothofagus moorei*), Queensland. The atmosphere is one of antiquity in this incredibly beautiful forest of moss-covered methuselahs, thought to be around 3000 years old

Left:
Karri trees (*Eucalyptus diversicolor*), south-west Western Australia. In the Warren National Park near Pemberton, early morning fog is chased away by the rising sun. This scene is along the Maidenbush Trail, a narrow one-way loop track that winds for about 7 kilometres over hilly terrain through virgin Karri forest. The Karri tree requires a good rainfall for growth; consequently it will only be found in the areas of the south-west which receives more than 1000 millimetres annually

bark hang from the trunks and limbs, others curl and peel off in an untidy fashion.

There are about 600 species and varieties of eucalypts, and all but six are indigenous to Australia. Only about twenty-five species are found in the arid Outback regions, the majority occurring in forests and woodlands which receive a favourable rainfall. Compared with trees such as the oaks and conifers of the Northern Hemisphere, or even Tasmania's Huon Pine, the eucalypts have a relatively short life-span. Although the River Red Gum and the more durable hardwood Jarrah may live up to 1000 years, the Mountain Ash, for example, has a potential span of only 200 to 400 years.

Some of the eucalypts are the tallest hardwoods

in the world, the Mountain Ash being topped only by the Californian redwoods. In Victoria and Tasmania this magnificent ash sometimes exceeds 90 metres—reports made last century of these trees reaching to 122 metres were not verified, though one was accurately measured at 114 metres. The Mountain Ash forests around Marysville, Healesville, and in the Dandenongs' Sherbrooke Forest Park are superb, with their straight trunks soaring

Koala. The natural habitat of this endearing marsupial is confined generally to Victoria, the coastal forests of New South Wales, and parts of Queensland. This one was photographed in the Grampians, Victoria, early in the morning

Grampians Bauera (*Bauera sessiflora*). The Grampians, a series of ranges lying east of Melbourne in Victoria, is one of the country's richest floral regions, with over 800 different plants—about one-third of the State's whole indigenous flora. This showy Bauera is one of many plants unique to the Grampians

upwards, and tree ferns and brackens massed around their base. There really is no excuse for Melburnians not to enjoy these great trees: Sherbrooke Forest Park, with its many delightful walking trails is only about an hour's drive from the city. Near Healesville, where the Maroondah Highway climbs to the Black Spur, the road is flanked by some of the loveliest Mountain Ash forest in the country.

Western Australia has its giants, too. The Karri, found in a small area of high rainfall in the State's south-west corner, may reach a height of 90 metres. Probably the most famous Karri is the Gloucester Tree near Pemberton, a fire lookout which has a small hut perched like a pinhead at the top of its 60-metre high bulk. Tourists may have the questionable pleasure of climbing the ladder wrapped around this 300-year-old tree, and thousands make the ascent in safety every year. But remember, the hut does sway in the wind! The Warren National Park, also near Pemberton, possesses some of the finest virgin Karri forest, and a drive along the Maidenbush Trail is a 'must'. Sometimes the forest is heavily blanketed in fog, which slowly lifts as the sun strengthens, giving the Karri trees, veiled in gossamer-like mist, an almost ethereal appearance.

Eucalypt forests all over the country harbour some of our most unique birds and animals. Of all the birds, the most spectacular is the Superb Lyrebird, inhabiting the forests of south-eastern Australia. They are astonishing mimics, and have even been known to confound foresters by faithfully reproducing the sounds of axe-blows and cross-cut saws. The male has a large and incredibly beautiful tail which he uses in an entertaining courtship display, spreading it wide like a fan while singing and dancing on a mound of scratched earth.

Without the gums, there would be no Koalas, for these animals will only eat the leaves of about twelve species of eucalypt, consuming around a kilogram a day. In their natural environment they are confined mostly to the forests of Victoria, coastal New South Wales, and parts of Queensland. Koalas are nocturnal, spending almost all their time in trees, and can bite and scratch when handled. One of the most surprising features of the Koala is the harsh call of the adult male. Campers often hear them at night in the Grampians, and the ignorant could well be rather alarmed if out of the nearby tree erupts a noise that sounds remarkably like a motorcycle with a broken exhaust.

Bunya Pine (*Araucaria bidwillii*), Queensland. A pillar of the rainforest, this Bunya Pine soars to the sky in order to reach the light above the forest's dense canopy. Endemic to southeast Queensland, this pine was milled extensively last century, and today the Bunya Mountains is the only area left where natural Bunya Pine forests still stand. These pines are now protected in a national park with many delightful walking paths

LAKES AND RIVERS

When a continent is as dry as Australia, its lakes and rivers are particularly valuable. The vital watershed for nearly half the country is the Great Dividing Range: from its slopes run many rivers and streams, born of melting snows in the south and tropical rains in the north. Many of these watercourses feed lagoons, lakes, and man-made dams, while others cascade as waterfalls for a brief moment somewhere along their course before reaching the plains. With their lakes and waterfalls, these rivers encompass some of Australia's most timeless beauty and varied moods.

On the eastern side of the Great Divide, after nourishing the relatively small area of fertile land between the ranges and the coast, a multitude of rivers pour into the Pacific Ocean. Although most of them only have comparatively short journeys over the plains before reaching their estuaries, many are broad and noble streams. On the north coast of New South Wales, the majestic Clarence River gives the district around Grafton and Maclean the name of 'Big River Country'. Anyone who drives alongside the Clarence River in this area, and then sees it near the coast at Yamba, spreading into a vast estuary with a complex network of channels, lagoons, and islands, must agree that it is a very appropriate name for the region.

From the western slopes, rivers carry their life-giving waters far out to the arid plains of the Outback, often reaching areas that have a pitifully low rainfall, then peter out into the sandy deserts or salt-pans. Cooper Creek is the classic example. Rising as the Thomson River at the western edge of the Great Dividing Range in north Queensland, it becomes the Cooper at the junction of the Thomson and Barcoo. By the time it reaches South Australia it is nothing more than a river of sand linked to a string of lakes and waterholes, some permanent, others drying out soon after the river stops flowing. The Cooper will only flow to its lower South Australian reaches after exceptionally heavy rains in the Queensland catchment areas. When this happens, its waters spill over the banks to feed a maze of shallow channels and billabongs, and for a

time may cover the land for hundreds of kilometres before reaching its final destination, Lake Eyre's great expanse of salt. This may only occur every fifteen to twenty years—or as in the mid-1970s, several years running. For both pastoralists and travellers, these are wonderful years.

Fortunately not all the rivers that flow westward from the Great Divide behave like Cooper Creek. Australia's greatest and most important river, the Murray, rises on the slopes of The Pilot in the Snowy Mountains of New South Wales, and travels 2570 kilometres before flowing into the Southern Ocean near Goolwa in South Australia. For three-quarters of its journey it marks the border between New South Wales and Victoria. Together with its vast network of tributaries, the Murray River drains more than one-fifth of the continent. Irrigation from this great river has now comfortably established thousands of hectares of fertile farmland in the Riverina—an area once largely sunburnt and arid.

The Murray is a river full of character and rich delights for the people who explore it. Before it reaches the plains, this great river is a fast running mountain stream of clear, icy water, frothing and bubbling over a stony river-bed that passes through dense forests. Access to the river at this point is not easy, but one spot that is ideal for picnics and trout fishing lies by the Alpine Way, near Tom Groggin. After leaving the wild and rugged mountain country the Murray becomes a meandering river with a strong and even dangerous current. Majestic river gums trace its journey over the Victorian plains, where the Murray spills into large numbers of billabongs, swamps, and marshes that teem with wildlife.

Once in South Australia, the river's character changes remarkably. Swollen with the waters of all its tributaries—including those of the great Darling River—the Murray sedately makes its way past a series of towering and colourful cliffs. In this region, between Renmark and Mannum, access to the river is easy, and its banks provide numerous secluded picnic and camping spots. It is a peaceful place,

The Murray River, near Berri, South Australia. For much of the river's journey through South Australia, it is lined with colourful cliffs like these ones at Springcart Gully between Berri and Renmark

and this tranquillity encourages us to savour the beauty of the river, and its timelessness. And when an old paddlesteamer passes by—carrying tourists, not cargo as in days gone by—one can reflect on the era of the riverboats that served towns, villages, and isolated farms along the river, before the arrival of the railways. Heavily burdened with silt and sluggish after its long journey, the Murray River loses much of its former beauty after Murray Bridge

as it broadens into Lake Alexandrina and Lake Albert, before blending its muddy waters with the fresh ocean surf.

The Darling River joins the Murray just below Mildura, after travelling for hundreds of kilometres under various names over the Outback plains from its source in the high country near Stanthorpe, Queensland. The Darling's flow has been much more reliable since it was dammed at Menindee— prior to this the river's flow would cease in times of drought, often leaving riverboats stranded for months. Looking at some particularly narrow and twisting stretches, it is hard to understand how the paddlesteamers could possibly have navigated it at all. Cluttered with debris from previous floods, the

roots of nearby river gums exposed on the steep, muddy banks, it looks an untidy river; yet still one senses a depth of character and charm that is peculiar to the Darling.

Many fishermen come here regularly—some over a span of twenty years or more—to fish for cod. Some of the old-timers complain bitterly that the days of good cod fishing are over, because the introduced carp is taking over the Darling. Carp may be entering a lot of Australia's streams, but the fishing is still good in many places. The British and other Europeans, who pay dearly for fishing rights if they can get them, find our licenses laughably easy to obtain. In Victoria for instance, a license to fish any river or lake within the State costs only a few dollars a year if you are over sixteen years of age; if you are under sixteen, no license is required at all.

Lacking a continental mountain chain like the Great Dividing Range in the east, Western Australia receives a much lower rainfall and consequently possesses few reliable major river systems. In the south-west a number of relatively small ranges give birth to several rivers, the most important being the Swan—Avon River, which rises on the Darling Plateau. Further north the Greenough and Murchison rivers survive on barely adequate winter rains, and the De Grey and Fortescue may not flow properly for years. In the tropical north-west, rivers rage in colossal floods during the annual wet season, only to become a string of waterholes by the end of the 'dry'.

The intermittent flow of these northern rivers does not detract from their loveliness; indeed, many of the waterholes are places of superb beauty. The Fortescue River has some idyllic long pools, shaded by magnificent stands of the paperbark melaleucas, river gums, and palms. In the northern areas of Western Australia adequate shade is all too rare, and after days of travelling over hot and dusty plains, it is an enormous relief to find spots like Crossing Pool on the Fortescue River, near Millstream Homestead.

In the Kimberleys, Joe's Waterhole is another superb resting-place for the weary traveller. Lying off the Gibb River Road in the wilderness country south-west of Wyndham, this waterhole is a large, permanent stretch of water on the Durack River, fringed with vegetation. On the breathlessly still

days at the end of the dry season, the mood of expectation in the hot air, and the great castles of cottonwool clouds towering in the sky, are reflected with extraordinary depth by the giant mirror of Joe's Waterhole.

For unusual beauty and a taste of adventure, there is Tunnel Creek, near Fitzroy Crossing in the far north-west. Here a watercourse runs through a 750-metre long cave which pierces the range at a spot close to the Windjana Gorge track. In the wet season water pours through the tunnel, but during the dry period one can walk right through to the other side of the range. A jumbled pile of splendid boulders, many musk-pink and intricately laced with white, almost block the entrance to the tunnel and access to the spacious cavern below. Here the utter silence and the dim light create an eerie atmosphere, and it is deliciously cool after the heat from outside. The blackness of the far reaches of the cavern—which leads to the rest of the tunnel—looks very uninviting when torches are reduced to candle strength in the heavy darkness, and you know that a chance meeting with a python or two is quite possible. The time of year determines how wet your feet get during the walk. Towards the end of the 'dry' there is usually enough sand or bare rock to walk over, but earlier on in the season pools stretch from wall to wall in places, and the ice-cold water can reach to waist level.

Despite this, the walk *is* worthwhile. Mid-way through the tunnel a partial collapse in the roof lets in sunlight, revealing an unusual and breathtaking beauty. Curving around the pile of rubble, the long pool reflects rocks, craggy walls, and tree roots dangling from the roof like streamers; nearby are stalagmites and stalactites. After the cave-in, you must walk on in blackness to reach the other end; the return journey is via the same route.

Rivalling the rivers and natural lakes in beauty are the many man-made dams. When rivers are trapped in mountain regions, the dams are often so beautiful it is hard to believe they are the result of technology. Lake Eildon in Victoria nestles among wooded slopes that are softly picturesque, while Lake Pedder in south-west Tasmania lies in an

The Darling River, between Wentworth and Pooncarie, New South Wales

Following pages:
Lake Menindee, New South Wales. Lying about 100 kilometres east of Broken Hill, this lake is the largest of a string of lakes fed by the Darling River. Now that it holds storage water for the Darling many trees have been drowned by the rising waters. This view was taken at sunset, in the Kinchega National Park

Lake Pedder, Tasmania. This man-made lake 170 kilometres south-west of Hobart was created by damming the Serpentine River—and flooding the much smaller, unique Lake Pedder. The new Lake Pedder is quite magnificent and is part of the South-West National Park, an untamed wilderness of craggy mountains, glacial lakes and tarns, and buttongrass plains.

untamed wilderness of craggy mountains, button grass plains, and glacial lakes. Lake Hume, damming the Murray River above Albury, has a special character, with its gentle emerald hills that change to a grassy yellow in summer. Most spectacular of all is the Ord Dam's Lake Argyle, nestling in the Kimberleys' Carr Boyd Ranges. Fed by the fast and furious floodwaters of the Ord River during the wet season, this lake gives the eastern Kimberleys a

new lease of life in the dry months, as well as a new dimension of astonishingly colourful beauty.

One of Australia's most unusual lakes is the Blue Lake at Mount Gambier, in the south-east of South Australia. One of four crater lakes in the area, the Blue Lake is distinguished for its dramatic overnight change in colour from grey to brilliant blue every November. However, the reason for the gradual change back to its dreary winter grey between March and June remains a mystery. And

Reedy Lake, near Kerang, Victoria. In the late afternoon light, the sun casts a sparkling path over the water. This is one of numerous lakes lying north of Kerang in the mid-Murray Valley. Some of the other lakes are breeding grounds for over 200 000 ibises

Nornalup Inlet, south-west Western Australia. This inlet is at its most beautiful when mists move over the water at sunrise. Together with Walpole Inlet, Nornalup forms part of the Walpole–Nornalup National Park, situated on the south coast, 121 kilometres from Albany.

unlike other stretches of water that on overcast days reflect the grey colour of the clouds, this lake retains its rich blue sheen. Strangely enough, Mount Gambier's other three crater lakes remain constant in colour all the year round. Another very beautiful lake that fills the mouth of a volcano is Lake Eacham, in north Queensland. Lying on the Atherton Tableland, this national park is extremely popular. However if you are there at dawn, or very late in the afternoon when no coaches are disgorging swarms of tourists, the atmosphere is almost unearthly in its peace and balmy tranquillity.

Whether man-made or natural, all lakes can be transformed into enchanting spectacles at dawn on a chill morning. Then their beauty is enhanced by a blanket of soft white mist that lingers over the still water until the gentle breezes accompanying the rising sun chase them away. Perhaps a sunrise or sunset over a lake is the most moving sight of all, when the sun casts its ephemeral stream of light over the sparkling water before slipping behind the horizon, allowing the after-glow to tint clouds and water alike from its palette of delicate pinks and reds.

Lake Eacham, Atherton Tableland, Queensland. This beautiful lake fills the mouth of an old volcano, and is one of several crater lakes in the district, evidence that this area was once subject to volcanic activity. Around the rim of the lake there is a shaded walking path which often dips down to the cool, still water

Millstream Falls, north Queensland. A tributary of the Herbert River, Millstream is one of Australia's widest waterfalls, spreading over 100 metres across the rocky escarpment after big rains. The falls lie in open woodland country on the western slopes of the Atherton Tableland, a few kilometres from Ravenshoe

Tunnel Creek, Western Australia. Lying off the Windjana Gorge track in the Kimberleys, Tunnel Creek offers some unique beauty for the more adventurous traveller. This is the rock fall section, lying about half way along the cave's tunnel, where part of the roof has collapsed

Above:
East Alligator River, Kakadu National Park, Northern Territory. This is upstream from Cahill's Crossing, about 290 kilometres east of Darwin, bordering the Arnhem Land Reserve. Here the river is tidal, and offers some excellent fishing—both for man and Saltwater Crocodiles. It is not an uncommon sight to see large crocodiles basking on the river banks

Right:
Lake Mokoan, near Glenrowan, Victoria. Sunset, with the air full of smoke from forest fires in the north-east of the State. Lying 9 kilometres from Glenrowan, Lake Mokoan is filled via an inlet channel from the Broken River. The water is stored for irrigation within the Murray River system

A GRAND COASTLINE

Australia's population is concentrated along its seaboard, and many people are caught in the spell of that wonderful combination of sea and shore. Come summer, thousands flock to city beaches, seaside resorts, and semi-wilderness coastal areas for sporting activities, sightseeing, or just lazing. Every winter, they again migrate, like the birds, from the southern regions to the considerably warmer northern coasts, in order to enjoy the same pastimes.

As the majority of Australians live on the eastern and south-eastern seaboard, access to much of this shoreline is relatively easy. However, in the north and much of the west, the coast is still largely inaccessible virgin territory. In the tropical north, extensive areas of mangroves and mud-flats, etched with winding rivers and creeks, stretch for many kilometres. Access to beautiful beaches is often impossible because of the difficult terrain lying immediately beyond the shores. Even more formidable is the Kimberley coastline in the far north-west, where the fragmented rocky shores are not only well guarded by an abundance of treacherous reefs and unpredictable tides, but also by an inland terrain indescribably wild and rugged.

The coastline runs for 38 000 kilometres around the continent, and contains an astonishing variety of beautiful scenery and interesting topographical features, of which the beaches are the most renowned. With names like Eighty Mile Beach and Ninety Mile Beach, they sweep unbroken towards distant horizons, wide and spacious, offering a freedom that is dear to the hearts of Australians. There is a multitude of smaller ones, stretching for only a few kilometres before meeting a headland, and many pocket-sized beaches, fitting snugly between piles of rocks or hiding between small coves. Great rolling waves wash many other stretches, sometimes capped with plumes of white spray, always the delight of surfboard riders. The gentle waters of other beaches are ideal for swimming and boating activities.

Around the coastline the colour of the sand varies from pure white through all shades of yellow and light brown to red. Nowhere are the sands as white as in south-western Australia. From Esperance to Cape Le Grand and Duke of Orleans Bay the coastal scenery is brilliant, dazzling white sands contrasting strongly with a sea that varies in colour from a pale aquamarine in the shallows, graduating through a series of rich blues to a deep navy further out. In places these white sands are so fine that they squeak underfoot, and when pressed in the hand feel like talcum powder. The treacherously fine sands of the Cape Arid region at the western end of the Great Australian Bight act like quicksand, capable of swallowing vehicles and men alike, and tragedies have occurred in this area.

In a few places on the north coast of Western Australia, red cliffs and dunes give way to white beaches, but at Broome, around Roebuck Bay, the dunes *and* the beach are red. In fact, redness is everywhere. Near the jetty, heaps of black and red rocks engraved with swirling patterns by weathering give way to a ribbon of red sand, gently lapped by the bright turquoise sea. Green bushes growing on the red dunes beside the beach add more splashes of colour. All this redness has an extraordinary air of unreality. A few kilometres from Broome's township one finds more vibrant colours at Gantheaume Point, where a profusion of red rocks sprawl into the colourful sea.

One of the joys of discovering Australia's coastline is its constant surprises—occasionally you may even find a place that doesn't seem to fit the Australian scene at all. One such place is the Pinnacles in Nambung National Park, situated about 250 kilometres north of Perth. On a wild and desolate coastal plain among undulating dunes almost devoid of vegetation, limestone spires rise like the ruins of an ancient and forgotten city. Some are grey in colour, but most of them are as golden as the surrounding sand, and range from the size of a man's hand to 5 metres in height.

These strange formations developed when limestone formed around the roots of trees and plants many thousands of years ago when the climate in this region was much wetter. Erosion gradually

One of the Remarkable Rocks, Kangaroo Island, South Australia. With a coastline of 450 kilometres packed with exciting scenery, Kangaroo Island lies off the State's Yorke and Fleurieu peninsulas. Access from the mainland is by air or vehicular ferry which leaves from Port Adelaide. The Remarkable Rocks, resembling pieces of broken egg shell, lumps of potters' clay, and even modern sculpture, balance on top of a domed granite headland in the far south-west of the island

exposed the solid spires and a mass of tiny fossilised roots. These pinnacles are very similar to a group in the Sahara Desert that rise to heights of 580 metres. Visitors in the Nambung National Park must drive only on the one-way loop track in order to preserve areas where the sand's delicate crust of tiny fossilised roots is still intact. The park's best protection is the road leading in from the small town of Cervantes, because the last section is full of huge rocks guaranteed to stop most conventional vehicles.

Few people are not moved by the sheer drama of great vertical cliffs plunging dizzily to the ocean below, where powerful rollers heave against the bare cliff-face and boom hollowly in hidden caves and crevasses. A considerable portion of Australia's shoreline is bounded by cliffs, and those places with easy access are always popular with visitors. Port Campbell National Park in south-west Victoria has grown to be one of the country's greatest coastal attractions, and there is easy viewing along the road and from many lookout points. The park protects about 32 kilometres of coast east of Warrnambool, where sheer cliffs plunge to the waterline.

Eucla, Western Australia. In between the cliffs of the Great Australian Bight there are vast stretches of dunes, some reaching colossal heights. Originally they were anchored by vegetation, but by the end of the nineteenth-century armies of introduced rabbits had devoured enough of the plant cover to permit massive wind erosion. Today the dunes are slowly on the move, and have all but swallowed the ruins of the old telegraph station

These cliffs are riddled with caves, tunnels, and blowholes, and in places some of the vertically-walled headlands have been fashioned over the ages into archways and natural bridges by the action of pounding waves, with whole sections breaking off to form small islands. Towering residual stacks rise majestically up to 100 metres out of the sea, the most famous being the Twelve Apostles.

There are more intriguing landforms along the east coast of Tasmania's Tasman Peninsula. As well as an active blowhole, a wonderful arch, and some notable caves and chasms, there is a curious tessellated pavement which actually looks man-made. At the southern tip of the peninsula tower massive columns of dolerite, resembling great organ pipes. New South Wales has its share too, in the Royal National Park, near Sydney, and South Australia's Eyre Peninsula has many kilometres of high craggy rock-faces lining the west coast. At Point Labatt the cliffs give some protection to the only colony of sea-lions on the mainland. Although there is a track of sorts down the cliff-face, most people fear the initial scramble over the edge to reach the path below.

Roebuck Bay, Broome, Western Australia. This is near the jetty, where red sand dominates the scene. Broome lies in the far north-west of the continent, 2213 kilometres from Perth. Roebuck Bay is too dangerous for swimming because of the sharks, but there is safe swimming on the ocean side of the town at Cable Beach, where the water temperature is a pleasant 26°C

The most thrilling cliffs in the entire country face on to the Great Australian Bight, the great curve that sweeps for 1000 kilometres against the underbelly of the continent. Much of it is edged by the longest lines of unbroken cliffs in the world. The most accessible section is in South Australia, where the highway crosses the Nullarbor Plain and dips close to the coast, between the Nullarbor Homestead and the border there are six different vantage points for viewing the cliffs. The views are stunning, and frankly quite terrifying—especially when a north wind is blowing and trying to bowl you over the edge. In places the cliffs drop nearly 200 metres and present a spectacular, sheer wall as far as the eye can see. And there is no shortage of

notices warning of the dangerous overhangs which look horribly fragile when viewed from further along the edge. In places the cliffs give way to fantastic white sand-dunes that roll like gigantic waves along the shore. At Eucla it is possible to walk among them, and once away from the thousands of footprints around the old telegraph station, you feel as if you are entering a formidable desert.

For more gentle coastal scenery, there is the south coast of New South Wales. Known popularly as the 'Sapphire Coast', this is an area of coastal lakes, lagoons, and quiet inlets. Here forested slopes and rolling green hills meet the sea, and sandy beaches and rocky shores give way to river estuaries flourishing with oyster farms. There are also many attractive towns and villages, some clustered around beautiful bays and headlands with splendid views. This coast is fortunate in its climate, which is the most equable in Australia, and prompts many people to retire here.

One appealing place on this coast is Merimbula, a picturesque town scattered around a beautiful

Cliffs of the Great Australian Bight, South Australia. These are the longest line of unbroken cliffs in the world, stretching for around 200 kilometres. The Western Australian section of the Bight also features a long line of cliffs. The re-routing in the 1970s of the Eyre Highway, which links the eastern and western States, has enabled travellers to view the cliffs to excellent advantage from numerous lookouts along the way

inlet, 470 kilometres south of Sydney. Through the trees that line the roads meandering along the cliff tops and low hills, one can catch tantalising glimpses of lovely vistas. The town of Narooma, lying north of Merimbula, has a superb beauty unsurpassed on the 'Sapphire Coast'. Situated on a hilly peninsula between the beautiful Wagonga River and the sea, Narooma is dominated by the glorious scenery of the inlet and the excellent surf beach.

Queensland has its share of gentle shores too, in fact much of it is a tropical paradise, with a superb climate and palm and casuarina-fringed beaches lying at the foot of the Great Dividing Range's densely timbered mountains. The major attraction here is the Great Barrier Reef, which extends for 2000 kilometres from the Torres Strait in the north to just south of the Tropic of Capricorn, near Gladstone. Considered one of the great wonders of the world, this reef is more complex than its name suggests. It comprises a myriad of coral reefs, cays, atolls, lagoons, rocky islands, and deep-water channels, and is home for an enormous variety of marine life. The eastern edge of the reef has massive coral walls rising to 180 metres from the floor of the continental shelf, giving the entire north-eastern coast considerable protection from the heavy seas of the Pacific Ocean. Many of the islands were once peaks of mountains belonging to the mainland, now they are forest-clad and fringed with coral, adding tremendous beauty to the region. Some are holiday resorts, offering the entertainments one would expect in a tropical playground, as well as sightseeing around the reef itself.

There is a multitude of other islands fringing the Australian coast, most of them originating from the continent. The largest is of course, Tasmania, with an area of 63 000 kilometres. The smallest are mere rocky outcrops. Some have never known the presence of man; many shelter a considerable amount of wildlife, including a number of rare species.

The Blowhole, Eaglehawk Neck, Tasmania. This is one of several fascinating landforms lying on the Tasman Peninsula. When the swell of the ocean is strong, water booms with great force through a hole in the cliff, furiously spilling out into a small channel

Above:
The Pinnacles Desert, Western Australia. Lying on the coast in the Nambung National Park about 250 kilometres north of Perth, these strange limestone spires, of every possible shape and size, stand in their thousands. In some places the sand around them is held together by a crust of tiny petrified roots, which will disintegrate at the slightest touch. The very rocky track into the park affords this fragile environment its best protection

Right:
Soldier crabs, Tomaga River estuary, New South Wales. Just south of Batemans Bay on the State's south coast, the Tomaga River flows into the Pacific Ocean. Sometimes at low tide masses of these colourful little crabs can be seen scuttling through the mangroves

Left:
The Island Archway, near Port Campbell, Victoria. Formed by powerful waves eating into the weaker sections of the limestone cliffs, this island archway rises dramatically out of the sea. It lies close to the coastal gorge Loch Ard, where a ship foundered in 1878 with the loss of fifty lives. The Island Archway is part of the Port Campbell National Park

Above:
Brampton Island, Queensland. Lying at the far southern end of the Whitsunday Passage, 32 kilometres from Mackay, beautiful Brampton Island is one of Australia's most popular holiday resorts. The long-established resort offers many facilities, including an airstrip and a deep-water jetty. This view is from the 6-kilometre Circuit Track, with flowering Yaccas in the foreground

Sunset from the Brampton Island resort

CITIES AND TOWNS

Australia is nearly the size of Europe (excluding Russia), yet in this space live 15 million people— about one-quarter of Great Britain's population. Perhaps the most surprising fact is that nearly 10 million Australians reside in the eight major cities— Canberra, Sydney, Melbourne, Brisbane, Adelaide, Perth, Hobart, and Darwin—and of these urban dwellers, two-thirds live in Sydney and Melbourne.

Settlement is mostly confined to the well-watered, fertile, eastern and south-eastern coast, where five of the seven State capitals lie, as well as the country's largest provincial cities. Most Australian cities are similar in that their relatively small central area is marked with a group of glinting high-rise buildings that tower over the older edifices and a fashionable new mall. Sprawling beyond the inner city are the industrial and residential suburbs, the latter expanding further each year as new estates cater for the great Australian dream of a fenced-off plot of land with a house and garden.

The national capital, Canberra, lies in the Australian Capital Territory, 304 kilometres south-west of Sydney and only a couple of hours' drive from the east coast. The only city to grow out of the twentieth century, Canberra is quite unique. It was established in 1911 and built to a specified plan which centred around Lake Burley Griffin, an artificial lake created especially for the city by trapping the waters of the Molonglo River. Today it is Australia's largest inland city with a population of around a quarter of a million. It continues to grow —both in population and in elegance. With its magnificent public buildings and monuments, parks, gardens, and the lake, all set in the hills of the Great Dividing Range, there is a pronounced air of prosperity and affluence not seen in any other Australian city. Of all the buildings, the most stirring is the Australian War Memorial, which houses a huge collection of war relics, paintings, and dioramas.

Sydney is the oldest and largest city. In January 1788 a party of British soldiers and convicts landed at Sydney Cove to establish a penal colony, marking the beginning of European settlement in Australia. From the troubled early days at Port Jackson grew the dynamic city we know today as Sydney, capital of New South Wales. With a population of around 3·25 million, it is the busiest port in the South Pacific, boasting one of the world's most magnificent harbours. Of all the cities in Australia, its pace of living would be the fastest—certainly visitors from the quieter capitals will tell you that the traffic borders on the frenetic, and that even the people walk more quickly. Fortunately there are many beautiful places that offer refuge from the hectic bustle. Lying off the busy main roads on the North Shore are leafy suburbs where kookaburras laugh and other lovely bird calls ring out. Around the harbour inlets and estuaries, there are many glorious spots offering peace and tranquillity, and there are even some National Parks lying within Greater Sydney.

Melbourne, the capital of Victoria, was one of the few big cities to be founded as a free settlement rather than as a penal colony. Two decades after its founding in 1835, the small village was thriving on the abundant amounts of gold found in the State. During the gold-rush era, Melbourne fast became a beautiful city, graced with wide, tree-lined streets, impressive buildings, and spacious parks and gardens. After the boisterous prospecting days had run their course, the city settled down to become a gracious and dignified metropolis, with a conservative air not found in the big city to the north. Today, with a population of around 3 million, Melbourne still retains its graciousness, and a touch of conservatism. It is the only Australian city to have hosted the Olympic Games, and was the first in declaring a public holiday to celebrate a horse race—the famous Melbourne Cup. It is also the only city in Australia that can offer a taste of all four seasons in one day.

Brisbane, the capital of Queensland, was founded in 1823 and built around the Brisbane River—now the largest commercial river in the country. Lying close to the New South Wales border and with a

The Opera House, Sydney, New South Wales

population of over 1 million people, Brisbane basks in a sub-tropical climate, and like so many cities and towns in Queensland, is friendly, easy-going, and casual to a degree that often baffles southerners. At its southern doorstep lies Australia's wealthiest playground—the Gold Coast—where fabulous homes line the still waters of man-made canals, and concrete jungles of luxury high-rise apartments tower over the sweeping sandy beaches.

Founded in 1836, Adelaide is South Australia's capital, and although it has a population similar in size to that of Brisbane, the city appears smaller than its sprawling Queensland sister; certainly Adelaide is more orderly and tidy, and with its well-designed road system motorists find it a trauma-free city. Overall Adelaide is a relaxing place, and it is fitting that this very attractive city's most notable distinction is its promotion of the arts. Every two years it holds what has been recognised as Australia's most important cultural festival, the Festival of Arts.

On the west coast of the continent, 2740 isolated kilometres from Adelaide, is Perth, the capital of Western Australia. After a great struggle to survive the initial founding of the colony in 1829, and despite its isolation from the urban east, Perth has grown into a thriving city around the banks of the Swan River, with a population reaching towards the million mark. Some people will tell you that this lovely city's best assets are the 400 hectares of beautiful native bushland that overlooks its heart, and the friendly, hospitable Western Australian inhabitants.

Adelaide, South Australia. The inner city's Victoria Square with its beautiful fountain, is a delightful refuge for busy city workers and shoppers

Alice Springs, Northern Territory. Lying almost in the dead centre of the continent, with the cities of Darwin 1534 kilometres to the north and Adelaide 1687 to the south, Alice Springs is the hub of central Australia. This view is from Anzac Hill, overlooking the town centre and beyond to Heavitree Gap, through which squeeze a river, road, railway, and telegraph line

Even more isolated than Perth is Darwin, at the tropical end of the Northern Territory. Indeed, there is little else in the way of settlement along the inhospitable northern seaboard. Compared with Australia's other cities, the capital of the Northern Territory is more like a big country town, yet Darwin has one of the highest growth rates in the country. It was virtually rebuilt after Cyclone Tracy devastated the city in 1974, but reconstruction was not a new experience for Darwin. It has been necessary on three previous occasions: after two earlier cyclones, and following the bombing by the Japanese in 1942. In 1969 the city celebrated its centenary with all the usual gusto Darwinians show for living. It is a hot place, yet the lifestyle is a comfortable one. Many visitors now pass through Darwin because it is the gateway to the Territory's exciting hinterland, and also to Asia.

The island State of Tasmania has Hobart as its capital. Although it only has a small population of 150 000, Hobart, settled in 1804, is Australia's second oldest city. Scenically it is magnificent, as the city nestles in the rolling hills by the beautiful Derwent River, guarded by majestic Mount Wellington. The capital and the entire island are rich in history, and fortunately many of the historic sites have been preserved, attracting thousands of visitors each year.

Many of Australia's provincial cities are steadily expanding. With a population of over 142 000 Geelong in Victoria is nearly the size of Hobart, and Newcastle in New South Wales is larger still, with almost 300 000 people. Some of Queensland's northern cities are mushrooming in

development, and places like Cairns are starting to feature high-rise buildings. In central Australia, Alice Springs has evolved from a rough and dusty village to a modern township, yet retains its distinctively Territorian character. No other town races camels in a Camel Cup, or holds a regatta in a dry, sandy river bed, using boats powered only by human legs, calling it the 'Henley-on-Todd'.

The small towns and villages possess some of the greatest interest and character to be found in Australia's urban areas. Many have retained a delightful colonial flavour, while some resemble settings from old Hollywood western movies. Others are charmingly quaint. A visit to Cooktown in far north Queensland, which has retained so many old buildings from its rollicking gold-rush days, is like taking a step back into history. It is the same with

Cairns, Queensland. Nestling in the foothills of the Atherton Tableland on the north-east tropical coast of Queensland, 1863 kilometres from Brisbane, Cairns is one of the fastest growing cities in the State. Thousands of Australians flock here to escape the cold southern winters, while the excellent big-game fishing draws overseas tourists

Broome, on the north-west coast of Western Australia, where the town's strong oriental influence is a reminder of the heyday of pearling. If visitors are fortunate enough to arrive at the time of Shinju Matsuri—the Festival of the Pearl—they will be able to sample even more of Broome's wonderful charm and fun.

One of the loveliest of all the country towns is Bright. Nestling in the foothills of the Victorian Alps, this small town comes into its own when its tree-lined streets, and its streams, parks, and private gardens blaze with the glory of autumn. Often the beauty is enhanced on fine, sunny days when a little early morning mist drapes the surrounding mountains, giving the town an almost magic quality. With its abundance of fresh mountain air and relaxed atmosphere, Bright is a wonderful refuge from the busy cities.

Below:
Melbourne, Victoria. From the steps of the Shrine in St Kilda Road, there are expansive views over the inner city and the parklands around the Shrine

Right:
Canberra, Australian Capital Territory. The marble-columned National Library is seen through the misty spray of the Captain Cook Waterjet, which spouts up to 137 metres before tumbling into the waters of Lake Burley Griffin

The historic church ruins at Port Arthur, Tasmania. This once notorious penitentiary is now an important historic site, with its many ruined buildings lying peacefully in picturesque parkland and drawing thousands of visitors every year. It lies on the Tasman Peninsula, beyond Eaglehawk Neck—the extraordinarily narrow isthmus that presented a natural 'gate' where guards could intercept would-be escapees from the penal settlement further south